FLOWER GARLANDS & CIRCLES

How to create 30 stunning displays with fresh and dried flowers

FIONA EATON

LORENZ BOOKS

This edition is published by Lorenz Books,
an imprint of Anness Publishing Ltd,
Blaby Road, Wigston, Leicestershire LE18 4SE;
info@anness.com

www.lorenzbooks.com; www.annesspublishing.com

If you like the images in this book and would like to investigate using
them for publishing, promotions or advertising, please visit our website
www.practicalpictures.com for more information.

Publisher: Joanna Lorenz
Editor: Fiona Eaton
Jacket design: Nigel Partridge
Contributors: Fiona Barnett, Kally Ellis, Tessa Evelegh,
Lucinda Ganderton, Terence Moore, Ercole Moroni, Pamela Westland
Photographers: James Duncan, Michelle Garrett, Nelson Hargreaves

PUBLISHER'S NOTE
Although the advice and information in this book are believed to be
accurate and true at the time of going to press, neither the authors nor
the publisher can accept any legal responsibility or liability for any
errors or omissions that may have been made nor for any inaccuracies
nor for any loss, harm or injury that comes about from following
instructions or advice in this book.

CONTENTS

INTRODUCTION

Wreaths and garlands are frequently among the most impressive of displays, whether draped over a fireplace or hung as a grand welcome on a front door or garden gate. From the simplest circle of twigs to the most extravagant of swags, perhaps festooned with fruit, their outlines and shapes have great visual impact.

These pages will show you how to create 30 different-sized designs to suit every occasion and situation. Arranged by season, this book contains a mix of fresh and dried flower designs that will enhance any occasion. If you are new to flower arranging, there are plenty of simple projects to get you started, and many of the displays will appeal to more experienced flower arrangers.

If you want a satisfying hobby that will deck your halls with wreaths and garlands, and fill your home with fragrance, colour and texture, this inspirational volume is perfect.

EASTER WREATH

*Easter is a time of hope and regeneration, and this bright Easter wreath
visually captures these feelings. The vibrant colours and the flowers, arranged
to look as though they are still growing, give the wreath a fresh, natural glow.*

MATERIALS

*30cm (12in) diameter plastic
foam ring
elaeagnus foliage
scissors
5 polyanthus plants
8 pieces of bark
stub (floral) wires
70 stems daffodils
3 blown eggs
2 enamel spoons
raffia*

1 Soak the foam ring in water
and arrange an even covering
of elaeagnus stems, approximately
7.5cm (3in) long, in the foam. At five
equidistant positions, add groups of
three polyanthus leaves.

2 Wire each piece of bark by
bending a stub (floral) wire
around the middle and twisting to
achieve a tight grip, Position the
pieces of bark equidistantly around
the ring using wires.

3 Arrange the polyanthus flowers
in single-coloured groups. Leave
a gap for the eggs and spoons. Cut
the daffodils to a stem length of
about 7.5cm (3in) and arrange them
between the polyanthus, pushing
their stems into the foam.

4 Wire the enamel spoons. Position
them in the gap in a cross. Wrap
raffia around the blown eggs, then
wire them carefully. Arrange the
remaining polyanthus flowers
and daffodils around the eggs and
crossed spoons.

ROSE HEART WREATH

This effective heart would make an unusual and long-lasting
Valentine's day gift.

stub (floral) wires
florist's (stem-wrap) tape
scissors
50 stems dried red roses
silver wires

1 Make a stay wire from stub (floral) wire on which the decoration can be built. Cover with florist's (stem-wrap) tape. Form the stay wire into a heart shape about 22cm (8¾in) high, the two ends of the wire meeting at its bottom point.

2 Cut the stems of the dried roses to a length of approximately 2.5cm (1in) and double leg mount them individually on silver wires, then tape the wired stems with florist's (stem-wrap) tape to hide the wire.

TIP

A double leg mount is a way of lengthening the stem with floral wires. With one-third of the wire to one side of the stem, start the wire one-third of the way up from the bottom of the stem. Then bend the wire so that it is parallel to the stem, so that one leg of the wire is twice the length of the other. With the shorter end against the stem, wrap the longer wire around stem and wire until firm.

3 Starting at the top, tape the rose stems to the stay wire. Slightly overlap the roses to achieve a continuous line of heads, finishing at its bottom point. Starting back at the top, repeat the process around the other half of the heart. Tape the two ends of the wire together.

MAY DAY WREATH

It's an old Greek custom to hang a colourful floral wreath, a stefani, on the door in celebration of the May Day festival. The decorations are composed of rings made of grass or other supple stems bound with a medley of wild and garden flowers. It is an idea well worth adopting for any occasion – just think what a warm welcome a flower ring would signal to party guests.

MATERIALS

scissors
a handful of supple grass or other
stems such as sheep's parsley
(Queen Anne's lace) and bryony
green binding twine
8 stems marigolds
5 stems pink roses
6 stems irises
6 spray chrysanthemums
20 sprays box foliage
florist's silver roll wire

TIP

If the stems you cut to make the ring are too rigid to shape into a circle, soak them in water, then hang them into a bunch to dry. When dry, the stems should be supple enough to shape into a ring.

1 Cut the grass stems to the length you require. To make a ring 30cm (12in) diameter, use stems 100cm (40in) long. Gather them into a neat bundle and pull out any that are particularly wayward. Wrap the twine around the stems, tie it into a knot and bind it over and around them. Overlap the ends to form a circle and tie securely.

2 Sort the flowers into groups, those which will be bound into posies and others which will be added individually. Mix and match the marigolds, roses, irises and spray chrysanthemums to give the posies a colourful and informal effect. Cut short the stems of the posy flowers and foliage and bind them with silver roll wire.

3 Using green twine or silver wire, bind on the posies and the individual flowers at random, so that the flowerheads cover the stems and binding of the one before. Continue binding on flowers to complete the colourful circle. It is not necessary to conceal every scrap of the stem ring, since it is a natural and authentic component of the finished design.

PROVENÇAL HERB HANGING

Fix bunches of fresh herbs to a thick plaited rope, add tiny terracotta pots to
give the design structure and then fill it in with garlic and colourful chillies to
make a spicy, herbal gift full of Provençal flavour, for anyone who loves to cook.

MATERIALS

scissors
hank of seagrass rope
garden string
florist's silver roll wire
fresh sage
fresh thyme
fresh oregano
2 small flowerpots
stub (floral) wires
2 garlic heads
large dried red chillies

1 Cut six lengths of seagrass rope about three times as long as the desired finished length of the hanging. Take two lengths, fold them in half and place them under a length of garden string. Pass the cut ends over the string and through the loop of the fold, thereby knotting the seagrass on to the garden string. Repeat twice with the remaining four seagrass lengths. Divide the seagrass into three bundles of four lengths and plait them to form the base of the herb hanging.

2 Finish the end of the plait by binding it with a separate piece of seagrass rope.

3 Using florist's silver roll wire, bind the herbs into small bundles and tie each one with garden string. Use this to tie them to the plait.

4 Wire the flowerpots by passing two stub (floral) wires through the top of the pot, through the central hole and then twisting the ends together on the outside.

5 Wire the pots to the base by passing a stub (floral) wire though the wires on the pots, then passing it through the plait and twisting the ends together.

6 Tie garden string around the garlic heads and tie these to the base. Wire the chillies into position, and fill the pots with more chillies.

MIDSUMMER HAY RING

Celebrate the height of summer with a dried flower hay ring composed of all the bright and beautiful colours of the rainbow. It can be hung as a brilliant party welcome on a gate, or an outside wall, or use it as a table decoration.

MATERIALS

green twine
25cm (10in) diameter copper wire ring
bundle of dry hay, or dry sphagnum moss
selection of colourful dried flowers such as sea lavender, statice, cornflowers, strawflowers and carthamus
scissors
florist's silver roll wire
wire cutters
stub (floral) wires
ribbons in toning colours

TIP

The ring may be completely covered with posies, or a section of the hay or moss may be left uncovered as a textured feature.

1 Tie the twine to the outer circle of the ring. Place handfuls of hay or moss over the ring and bind it on securely with the twine.

3 Cut several stub (floral) wires in half and bend them to make U-shaped staples. Place a posy over the covered ring, loop a staple over the stems and press into the hay or moss. Bend back the wire ends and twist them around the back of the wire ring to secure.

2 Gather the flowers into small, colourful mixed posies. Cut the stems short and bind them with florist's silver roll wire.

4 Continue fixing more posies around the ring so that the heads of each one cover the stems of the one before. Alternate the colours for the brightest effect. Fold the ribbon lengths in half and attach them to the ring with a stub (floral) wire.

CONTEMPORARY WREATHS

These two wall-hanging decorations show how massed dried flowers in strong contrasting colours can create a striking contemporary display.

MATERIALS

FOR THE RED AND YELLOW WREATH
scissors
34 stems dried red roses
33 stems dried yellow roses
glue
10cm (4in) diameter plastic foam ring
for dried flowers
ribbon

FOR THE BLUE AND WHITE WREATH
scissors
25 stems white roses
26 small heads blue globe thistle
glue
10 cm (4 in) diameter plastic foam ring
for dried flowers
ribbon

TIP
Alternative materials can be used to make these wreaths, provided the flowerheads used in any display are all about the same size.

1 For the red and yellow wreath, cut the rose stems to 2.5cm (1in). Around the outside edge of the foam ring, form a circle of alternating yellow and red roses by gluing their stems and pushing them into the foam. Leave a small gap in the rose circle for a ribbon.

2 Inside the first circle, construct a second circle, offsetting the colours against the first ring. Continue building circles of roses until the ring is covered. Pass the ribbon through the ring to hang the wreath, or tie it in a bow. Follow the same method for the second wreath.

GLOBE THISTLE AND MUSSEL SHELL RING

This display is strongly evocative of the seaside. The spiky globe thistles contrast with the smooth hard surface of the mussel shells and the most memorable feature of the display is its beautiful blue colouring.

MATERIALS

9 half mussel shells
13cm (5in) diameter plastic foam ring
for dried flowers
glue gun
scissors
65 globe thistle heads of various sizes

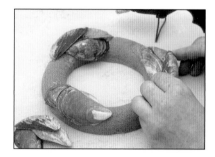

1 Position groups of three slightly overlapping mussel shells at three equidistant points around the ring. Glue them to the plastic foam and to each other.

2 Cut the globe thistle stems to around 2.5cm (1in) long, put a small blob of glue on the stems and push them into the plastic foam. Continue until the foam is covered.

TIP
The ring would look wonderful displayed in either a bathroom or a kitchen.

SMALL FRESH ROSE RING

While this delightful floral circlet could be used at any time of the year,
the impact created by the massed red roses makes it particularly romantic. It can
be hung on a wall or, with a candle at its centre, used as a table decoration for a
celebratory dinner for two.

MATERIALS

15cm (6in) diameter plastic foam ring
dark green ivy leaves
stub (floral) wires
bun moss
scissors
20 stems dark red roses

1 Soak the plastic foam ring in water. Push individual, medium-size ivy leaves into the foam to create an even foliage outline all around the ring.

2 Make U-shaped staples out of the stub (floral) wires and pin small pieces of bun moss on to the foam ring between the ivy leaves. Do this throughout the foliage.

TIP

If you receive a bouquet of red roses, why not recycle them? After the rose blooms have fully blown open, cut down their stems for use in this circlet to extend their lives. Finally dehydrate the circlet and continue to use it as a dried flower display.

3 Cut the rose stems to about 3.5 cm (1½in) long and push them into the foam until the ring is evenly covered. The ivy should still be visible in between the rose heads.

CELEBRATION TABLE GARLAND

*A garland is a lovely way to decorate a wedding or christening reception,
a birthday, or other celebration. The garland, composed of long leafy
stems, can be made to loop across the front-of the buffet table,
or to drape on all four sides of a free-standing table.*

MATERIALS

scissors
gypsophila
mimosa
white spray chrysanthemums
tape measure
florist's silver roll wire
bundle of smilax (Asparagus
asparagoides) foliage
pin
ribbon

1 Cut the flower stems short, then make up the posies, using five pieces of gypsophila, two snippings of mimosa, and one or two spray chrysanthemums. Bind the stems with silver roll wire.

2 Space the posies as close together or as wide apart as desired. As a general rule, the smaller the table the smaller the gap should be between the flowers. Measure the length of garland needed and mark the centre.

3 With the stems of the first posy facing towards the end of a length of smilax, bind the posy to the main stem with silver roll wire. Bind on more posies in the same way, reversing the stems' direction from the centre of the garland.

4 Continue adding posies to the remaining lengths of garland, but do not reverse the direction of the flowers of the side trails. Pin the garland to the cloth, so that it is equal on all sides, and pin on the side trails. Pin ribbon or bows to the corners and the centre of the drapes.

LAVENDER WREATH

*Lavender is an important plant in the traditional cottage garden and has
been widely cultivated over centuries for the perfume of its purple flowers.*

MATERIALS

*natural seagrass rope or coarse string
30cm (12in) diameter twig wreath
dried lavender sprigs*

1 Tie one end of the seagrass rope
or string securely to the wreath.

2 Hold a bunch of lavender across
the wreath with the flowers
pointing outward. Wind the rope or
string around the stalks and the
wreath to spiral-bind them in place.

TIP
The healing powers of lavender
are used in aromatherapy to ease
headaches and stress, and this
wreath will fill any room in which
it hangs with the rich scent
of summer.

3 Place a second lavender bunch to
the right of the first, and bind in
place with the rope or string. The
next bunch goes to the right of the
second, with the flowers pointing
away from the wreath.

4 Continue to spiral-bind small
bunches until the twig wreath
is completely covered. Tie off the end
of the rope or string and finish off
with a loop for hanging.

FRESH HERB WREATH

Gather together a basketful of sweet fresh herbs and make them into
an aromatic wreath, to hang in the kitchen or to use as a decorative
garland for a celebration.

MATERIALS

florist's silver roll wire
fresh sage
fresh or dried lavender
fresh parsley
glue gun
30 cm (12 in) diameter twisted
wicker wreath
fresh chives
scissors
raffia

1 Using the florist's silver roll wire, wire all the herbs except the chives into generous bunches.

2 Using the glue gun, attach two bunches of sage to the wreath base, stems pointing inward.

3 Next, attach enough lavender bunches side by side to cover the width of the wreath base, hiding the sage stems. Attach bunches of parsley to cover the lavender stems in the same way. Work around the wreath base in this way until it is generously covered with the herbs.

4 Wire the chives into four generous bunches and trim the cut ends straight. Form each pair into a cross and bind with raffia. Wire the crosses into position on the wreath.

5 Tie raffia around the wreath at intervals. Make a raffia hanging loop, thread this on to a generous bundle of raffia at the centre top, and tie the ends of the bundle into a bow to finish.

BRIDESMAID'S HOOP

This large-scale wreath is simplicity itself, and contributes a rustic feel to
a country wedding. The natural materials used make it equally suitable
for a younger bridesmaid or page boy.

MATERIALS

birch twigs
stub (floral) wires
ivy trails (sprigs)
rowanberries
Alchemilla mollis
scissors
florist's (stem-wrap) tape

TIP

This design can be scaled down to make a bridesmaid's headdress, which would complete the country feel of the ensemble.

1 Twist a few pieces of birch twig around one another, staggering and bending them into shape as you go. Bind any weak spots with wire.

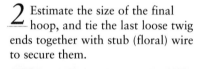

2 Estimate the size of the final hoop, and tie the last loose twig ends together with stub (floral) wire to secure them.

3 Wrap the ivy trails (sprigs) loosely around the hoop to cover it almost completely and evenly. Do not be sparing. Ensure that all the wired points are hidden by the ivy.

4 Wire generous groups of rowanberries together and tape them. Push these through the hoop at regular intervals. Repeat using wired bunches of *Alchemilla mollis*.

SUMMER WEDDING TABLE GARLAND

This is just about the simplest possible garland to make, but used as a table-edge decoration hanging in short loops it gives an impressive finish to the top table or cake table. Pale pink roses are used here for a summer wedding, but you could change the rose colour to give a different feel: red roses mixed with the conifer and used on a dark background would create a wintry look; for spring, pale yellow roses could be used.

MATERIALS

tape measure
scissors
rope
fresh conifer
florist's silver roll wire
pale pink roses

TIP

This design isn't long-lasting; the conifer will dry, become brittle and lose its vibrant green colour. If the garlands need to be made a few days before the event, hang them in a cool, dry, dark place; this will ensure that the conifer stays looking good and will leave time for other preparations. For a really fresh look, steam the roses to open them.

1 Measure the table edge and cut the rope to the required length. Make a loop at each hanging end. Trim the fresh conifer to short lengths and bind it firmly to the rope, covering it all the way round with florist's silver roll wire.

2 Continue this process, adding the pink rose stems in twos and threes, with a handful of conifer stems at regular intervals. Pack the conifer fairly tightly to produce a thick, luxurious garland.

SUNFLOWER RING EXTRAVAGANZA

This flamboyant garland celebrates the strong colour and echoes the dramatic circular shape of sunflowers. The sunflowers in this garland simply generate sunshine; even though the flowers are dried it has an abundant, fresh feel that will inject life into any environment.

MATERIALS

twine
25 cm (10 in) diameter copper ring
hay or moss
scissors
stub (floral) wires
selection of dried flowers such as Alchemilla mollis, amaranthus, blue larkspur, carthamus, eucalyptus, Nigella orientalis and sunflowers
twigs
florist's silver roll wire
glue gun

TIP

The garland can be adapted for other seasons – with the addition of brown preserved oak leaves and more eucalyptus, for example, it could be transformed into an autumnal display.

1 Tie the twine to the outer circle of the ring. Place handfuls of hay or moss over the ring and bind it on securely, taking the twine over and through the ring and pulling it tightly, to conceal it in the covering material. When the ring is completely covered, cut the twine and tie it to the ring.

2 Attach a stub (floral) wire to the covered ring, to create a loop with which to hang the finished garland. First bend the wire into a U-shape; then push it through the ring from the side which will become the back of the garland. Twist the ends of the wire together and tuck them neatly into the hay.

3 Separate the flowers and twigs into bunches and trim each stem so that it is about 20cm (8in) long. Lay the posies in position and wind florist's silver roll wire around to hold the stems tightly to the ring. Fill any spaces on the finished ring by gluing large-headed flowers, small bunches of flowers or hanks of moss, if using it, into the gaps.

FRUIT AND FLOWER SWAG

The colour and content of this decorative swag will brighten any room.
Its visual freshness makes it especially suitable for a kitchen but, if it were
made on a longer base, the decoration could be a mantelpiece garland, or
even extended to adorn the banister of a staircase.

MATERIALS

stub (floral) wires
4 limes
9 lemons
4 bunches black grapes
4 bunches sneezeweed (Helenium)
1 bundle tree ivy
straw plait (braid),
about 60cm (24in) long
raffia
scissors
1 bunch ivy trails (sprigs)

1 First, wire all the fruit. Pass a wire through from side to side just above the base of the limes, leaving equal lengths of wire projecting from either side, bend these down and twist together under the base. If the lemons are heavier than the limes, pass a second wire through them at right angles to the first, providing four equal ends to twist together.

2 Group the grapes in small clusters and double leg mount with stub (floral) wires. Then form 12 small bunches of sneezeweed mixed with tree ivy and double leg mount these on stub (floral) wires.

3 Starting at its bottom end, bind three wired lemons to the plait (braid) with raffia. Then in turn bind a bunch of flowers and foliage, a lime, grapes and a second bunch of flowers and foliage.

4 Continue binding materials to the plait in the above sequence until almost at the top. Secure by wrapping the remaining raffia tightly around the plait (braid).

5 Make a bow from raffia and tie to the top of the swag. Trim off any stray wire ends. Entwine the ivy trails (sprigs) around the top of the swag and bows.

ROSE AND STARFISH WREATH

*The design of this simple wreath involves massing a single type of flower
and framing them with a halo of geometric shapes, in this case stars.*

MATERIALS

*10 small dried starfish
stub (floral) wires
scissors
glue
13cm (5in) diameter plastic foam ring
for dried flowers
45 shell pink dried rose heads
velvet ribbon*

1 Double leg mount the starfish as
an extension of one of their arms
with a stub (floral) wire. Cut the
wire to about 2.5cm (1in) and
apply glue to both the tip of the
starfish arm and wire. Push the wired
arm into the outside edge of the
ring. Position all the starfish around
the ring. Leave a gap for the ribbon.

2 Cut the stems of the rose heads
to about 2.5cm (1in) and put glue
on their stems and bases. Push the
glued stems into the foam to
form a ring on top of the starfish.
Working towards the centre of the
ring, continue forming circles of roses
until the ring is covered, apart from
the gap for the ribbon.

TIP
The prettiness of this wreath's soft
peach colours makes it suitable for
a bedroom wall, in which case
sprinkle it with scented oil.

3 Pass the ribbon through the
centre of the ring and position
it so that it sits in the gap between
the roses and starfish to cover the
foam. This can be used to hang up
the wreath or just tied in a bow
for decoration.

HEART OF WHEAT

Fashion a heart at harvest time, when wheat is plentiful, for a delightful decoration that would look good adorning a wall or a dresser at any time of the year. Despite its delicate feathery looks, this heart is quite robust and should last many years.

MATERIALS

scissors
heavy-gauge garden wire or similar
florist's (stem-wrap) tape
florist's silver roll wire
large bundle wheat ears

1 Cut three long lengths of heavy-gauge wire and bend them into a heart shape. Twist the ends together at the bottom, and then use florist's (stem-wrap) tape to bind the wire to form a heart shape.

2 Using florist's silver roll wire, make up enough small bundles of wheat ears to cover the wire heart shape densely. Leave a short length of wire at each end for attaching to the heart shape.

3 Starting at the bottom, tape a bundle of wheat ears to the heart. Place each bundle further up the heart, shape and tape it in position. Continue until the whole heart is covered.

4 For the bottom, wire together about six bunches of wheat ears, and wire them to the heart, finishing off with florist's (stem-wrap) tape. This is what the finished back of the heart should look like.

AUTUMN FABRIC AND FLOWER SWAG

*This is an ideal swag for an entrance hall or lobby. The terracotta adds a rustic,
country touch to the piece. You could push small, tied bunches of
other materials into terracotta pots or fill them with autumn fruits such
as horse chestnuts.*

MATERIALS

*wire cutters
chicken wire
moss
pliers
terracotta flowerpots
stub (floral) wires
fabric
scissors
pins
glue gun
dried lavender
dried roses
dried peonies*

TIP
For a prettier, lighter look, use
pale-coloured chintz and summer
flowers, such as yellow solidago,
oregano and pale yellow roses, with
a little pale blue lavender.

1 Cut 70–90cm (2–3ft) of
chicken wire, roll it slightly and
fill with moss. Close up and fold in
the sharp edges with the pliers.

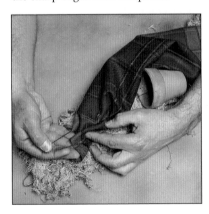

2 Attach terracotta pots at random
angles, by passing a stub (floral)
wire through the pot and the chicken
wire and twisting the ends together.

3 Fold a strip of fabric lengthways
into three to make a band about
10cm (4in) wide. Pin one end to
the top of the swag with a bent stub
(floral) wire. Wrap the fabric down
the length of the frame and around
the pots. At intervals secure the
fabric in place with a U-shaped wire.
The raw edges of the fabric should
always be at the back. Once
attached, go back and pull the fabric
into its final shape. Tuck the end
into the last terracotta pot and pin it.

4 Make a fabric bow and stick it to the top of the swag with the glue gun. Trim the lavender and roses to a length of 15cm (6in) and centre-wire them. Push the stub (floral) wire of each bunch into the frame. Push each bunch in randomly, criss-crossing the bunches until the whole frame and all the moss are covered. Cut the peony heads from their stems and glue them down the length of the swag. Fill any spaces with moss.

PRESSED LEAF RING

A ring of pressed autumn leaves and dried seed carriers makes an unusual and highly textured wall decoration. To protect the plant materials, place them behind glass in a frame, mount them on coloured cardboard and cover with transparent film, or display them under the glass top of a coffee table.

stiff cardboard
pair of compasses or plate and saucer to outline ring
pencil
scissors
clear glue
selection of pressed leaves and dried seedheads
small paintbrush, to move pressed leaves
piece of plain paper

1 Measure and draw the inner and outer rims of the ring on the cardboard, and cut it out. This design is 28cm (11in) in diameter. Make the selection of pressed leaves as varied as possible in both shape and colour.

TIP
The completed ring, which is an interpretation of a carpet of fallen leaves in a woodland, looks best mounted on colours in keeping with the autumnal theme. Choose muted greens, rich creams, clear greys, and burnt umber in preference to strong or primary colours, which may overshadow the subtle colour blend of the leaves.

2 Put small dabs of glue on to the tip, centre and stem end of each small leaf and arrange them, overlapping, so the tips extend beyond the inner and outer rims of the cardboard ring. Cover the leaves with a sheet of plain paper and press firmly with your hand. Put dabs of glue at intervals on the back of large and shapely leaves, place them on to the first layer, and press in place.

3 Continue to build up layers of leaves and seedheads so that the design is full of interest and contrast.

TEXTURED FOLIAGE RING

Some types of foliage can be successfully air dried but many others cannot and need to be glycerine preserved. This decoration mixes both types of foliage to create a feast of textures and subtle colours that succeeds without the enhancement of flowers.

MATERIALS

scissors
10 stems dried natural-coloured honesty
5 branches glycerine-preserved beech leaves
60cm (24in) length dried hop vine adiantum
5 branches glycerine-preserved 30cm (12in) diameter twisted wicker wreath twine

1 Cut all the foliage stems to around 12cm (5in) long. You will need 21 lengths of each type of foliage to cover your wicker wreath. Start by securely tying a group of three stems of honesty to the wreath with twine.

2 Making sure it overlaps the honesty, bind on a group of three glycerine-preserved beech stems with the same continuous length of twine. Repeat with three stems of hops followed by three stems of glycerine-preserved adiantum.

TIP
Very easy to construct from commercially available materials, this foliage ring makes a wonderful autumn wall decoration for a hall or, if protected from the weather, a front door.

3 Continue binding materials to the ring in the same sequence until the ring is completely covered. Cut off any untidy stems and adjust the materials to achieve the best effect. Finally, tie off the twine in a discreet knot at the back of the ring.

DRIED-GRASS HARVEST SWAG

This harvest swag is a symbolic collection of dried, decorative grasses.
It relies on the subtlety of colour differences and textural variation in the
grasses for its natural, yet splendid, effect.

MATERIALS

1 bunch dried, natural triticale
1 bunch dried, natural linseed
(flaxseed)
1 bunch dried, natural
Nigella orientalis
1 bunch dried, natural phalaris
scissors
stub (floral) wires
1 straw plait (braid),
about 60cm (24in) long
twine
raffia

TIP
Although a good deal of wiring is required for the construction of this swag, it is relatively straightforward and enjoyable to make.

1 Split each bunch of grass into 8 smaller bunches, giving you 32 individual bunches. Cut the stems to approximately 15cm (6in) long and double leg mount the individual groups with stub (floral) wires.

2 Start by tying a wired bunch of triticale to the bottom of the plait (braid) with the twine. Then place a bunch of linseed above, to the left and overlapping the triticale, and bind this with twine.

3 Follow this with a bunch of *Nigella orientalis* above, to the right, and overlapping the triticale. Finish the sequence by positioning a bunch of phalaris directly above the triticale, slightly overlapping it, and bind on with the twine. Repeat this pattern eight times using all four varieties of grass.

4 When all the grasses have been
used and the top of the plait
(braid) reached, tie off with the twine
and trim any excess wires.

5 Make a bow from the raffia
and tie it on to the top of the
decorated plait (braid), covering the
wires and the twine.

CRESCENT MOON WREATH

*This novelty decoration is designed to be hung on the wall of a nursery
or child's bedroom. The golden yellow of* Craspedia globosa *and the pale
gold sheen of the linseed seedheads give the decoration a luminosity
which children will love.*

MATERIALS

scissors
35 Craspedia globosa *heads*
silver wires
1 bunch dried linseed (flaxseed)
florist's (stem-wrap) tape
stub (floral) wires

1 Cut the *Craspedia globosa* heads to a stem length of approximately 2cm (¾in) and double leg mount them on silver wires. Split the dried linseed into very small bunches, each approximately 4cm (1¾in) long, and double leg mount them on wires. Tape all the wired materials with the florist's (stem-wtap) tape. Create a stay wire approximately 60cm (24in) long from the stub (floral) wires.

2 Cover the stay wire with florist's (stem-wrap) tape. Bend the stay wire into the outline of a crescent shape, taking care to ensure an even arc and pointed ends.

3 At one open end of the stay wire, tape on a bunch of linseed, then a small head of the *Craspedia globosa* slightly overlapping. Use the smaller heads of the *Craspedia globosa* at the pointed ends of the crescent and the larger heads at its centre. As you get toward the centre of the crescent, increase the width of the line of materials by adding material to the sides of the wire. Decrease the width again as you work towards the far point.

4 When the outside edge of the crescent outline has been completed, repeat the process on the inner edge but this time working from the bent point of the crescent down towards the open end of the stay wire. When the inner wire has been decorated, join the two open ends of the stay wire by taping them together, then cut off any excess wires and tape over their ends. This join will be hidden by the dried materials.

WINTER CONE GARLAND

*Take care when you are bending the larch twigs for this simple garland
that they do not break. Leave some of the small branches longer than you need,
so that they stick out from the ring to create interesting angles.*

MATERIALS

*wire cutters
copper wire ring
larch cones on twigs
stub (floral) wires
terracotta flowerpots
chillies
glue gun
moss
gold spray paint (optional)
rope or raffia*

1 Cut off the cross wires between the two copper rings and discard them. Cut the wire as close to the ring as possible. Use either of the copper rings, depending on the size you want.

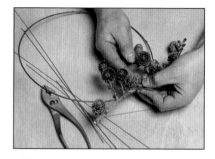

2 Tie a larch twig to the ring using a stub (floral) wire. Make sure the fixing is as near to one end of the twig as possible. Then, bending the twig gently to the shape of the ring, repeat the fixing on the other end of the twig.

3 Continue with this process until the whole ring is covered with larch twigs and cones. Where the twigs are small or thin, add more than one at a time, crossing the ends of the twigs over each other.

4 Centre-wire three bunches of chillies and attach them to the ring, twisting the loose ends together.

5 Attach the last bunch of chillies to the ring. Wire two terracotta pots to the ring in the same way. Glue on moss to cover the fixings. If wished, frost the garland with gold spray paint. Finish with a rope bow.

WISPY EVERGREEN RING

A bundle of wispy evergreens, clusters of gilded seedheads, a few sprigs of mistletoe and two glittering bows make this the prettiest yule-tide wreath ever.

MATERIALS

*wheat and linseed (flaxseed) seedheads
artificial Christmas roses
evergreens such as cypress, ivy,
mistletoe and eucalyptus
gold spray paint
florist's silver roll wire
secateurs (pruning shears)
scissors
stub (floral) wires
30cm (12in) diameter stem wreath
ribbon*

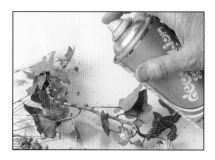

1 Spread out the wheat and linseed (flaxseed) seedheads, the artificial flowers, and any evergreens to be sprayed with gold paint. Spray the materials on one side, then turn over and spray on the other. Leave to dry.

2 Gather the wheat into small bunches and bind them with silver roll wire. Gather the linseed (flaxseed) into bunches of uneven lengths – this gives the finished outline a wispy look.

3 Cut the selected evergreens into short lengths. Cut several stub (floral) wires in half and then bend them over to make U-shaped staples. Place a bunch of evergreens over the stem wreath, loop a staple over the stalks and press the wire into the wreath base.

4 Take a bunch of wheat and a piece of mistletoe, place so the heads cover the evergreen stems and wire in place. Continue adding evergreens and other materials all around the ring, the heads of one cluster or bunch covering the stalks of the previous one.

5 Position the artificial flowers on the ring asymmetrically. You can push more stems horizontally through the evergreens and into the wreath base. Tie two bows with the ribbon, then push half a stub (floral) wire through the loop at the back of the bows and insert into the wreath.

TULIP AND HOLLY WREATH

The extravagant use of white tulips achieves a sophisticated purity in this Christmas decoration. A cushion of white blooms interspersed with glossy dark green leaves and vibrant red berries produces a wreath that can be used either on a door or, with candles, as a table centrepiece.

MATERIALS

*25cm (10in) diameter plastic foam ring
scissors
100 stems white tulips
holly with berries*

1 Soak the plastic foam ring in water. Cut the tulips to a stem length of approximately 3cm (1¼in). Starting at the centre, work outward in concentric circles to cover the whole surface of the plastic foam with the tulip heads.

2 Cover any exposed foam and the outside of the ring with holly leaves by pushing their stems into the foam and overlapping them flat against the edge of the ring.

3 Cut 12 stems of berries about 4cm (1¾in) in length and push them into the foam in two concentric circles around the ring, one toward the inside and the other toward the outside. Make sure no foam is visible.

TIP
The tulip stems are pushed fully into the foam in tight masses, so that only their heads are visible.

WINTER TABLE SWAG

The dominant material used in this festive swag is fresh blue pine (spruce).
After a few days it will begin to dry out, but it will keep its colour and
retain all its needles.

MATERIALS

scissors
rope
cutters
blue pine (spruce)
florist's silver roll wire
cones
chillies
stub (floral) wires
glue gun
mushrooms
pomegranates
reindeer moss
lavender
red roses

1 Cut two lengths of rope; their combined length should be the length you want the swag to be. Cut the blue pine (spruce) to about 20cm (8in) long. Bind the stems to the rope with florist's silver roll wire.

2 If some cones are attached to the stems, bind them to the rope with florist's silver roll wire and continue to add the pine (spruce).

3 Continue the process until the whole length of both ropes has been covered. Don't leave gaps along the edges as you add the pine (spruce) to the rope. Centre-wire the chillies with stub (floral) wire. Secure them along the length of the swag.

4 Glue the mushrooms, loose cones and pomegranates in place. Then add the reindeer moss.

5 Centre-wire the lavender and roses. Attach them in groups, crossing a bunch of roses with a bunch of lavender. Remember to twist the loose wires under the swag and to tuck the sharp ends back into the bottom of the swag.

TWIGGY DOOR WREATH

*Welcome seasonal guests with a door wreath that's charming in its
simplicity. Just bend twigs into a heart shape and adorn the heart with
variegated ivy, berries and a Christmas rose, or substitute any pure white rose.*

MATERIALS

*secateurs (pruning shears)
pliable branches such as buddleia, cut
from the garden
florist's silver roll wire
seagrass rope
variegated ivy trails (sprigs)
red berries
tree ivy
picture framer's wax gilt (optional)
white rose
golden twine*

1 Using secateurs (pruning shears)
cut six lengths of pliable
branches about 70cm (28in) long.
Wire three together at one end.
Repeat with the other three. Cross
the two bundles over at the wired
end. Wire the bunches together in the
crossed-over position.

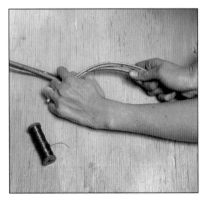

2 Holding the crossed, wired ends
with one hand, ease the long end
around and down very gently so the
branches don't snap. Repeat with the
other side, to form a heart shape.
Wire the bottom end of the heart.

3 Bind the wiring with seagrass
rope at top and bottom, and
make a hanging loop at the top.

4 Entwine trailing ivy around the
heart shape. Add berries. Make a
posy of tree ivy leaves (if you like,
gild them using picture framer's wax
gilt) and a white rose. Tie the posy
with golden twine. Wire the posy in
position at the top of the heart.

CLEMENTINE WREATH

This festive Christmas wreath is contemporary in its regular geometry and its
bold use of materials and colours. The wreath has a citrus smell, but can be
made more aromatic by using bay leaves and other herbs instead of ivy.

MATERIALS

stub (floral) wire
27 clementines
scissors
30cm (12in) diameter plastic
foam ring
pyracanthus berries and foliage
ivy leaves

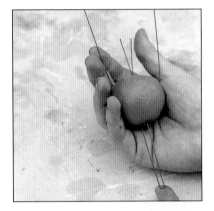

1 Push a stub (floral) wire across and through the base of a clementine from one side to the other, and bend the two projected ends down. Bend another wire to form a U-shaped staple and push the ends right through the middle of the clementine so that the bend in the wire is sitting flush with the top of the fruit. Do the same to all the clementines. Cut all the projecting wires to a length of approximately 4cm (1¾in).

2 Soak the plastic foam ring in water. Arrange the wired clementines in a tight circle on the top of the plastic ring by pushing their four projecting wire legs into the foam. Form a second ring of clementines within the first ring.

3 Cut the pyracanthus into small stems of berry clusters and foliage approximately 6cm (2¼in) long. Push the stems into the outer side of the plastic ring and between the two rings of clementines, making sure they are evenly distributed.

4 Cut the ivy leaves into individual stems measuring approximately 7cm (2¼in) in length. Push the stems of the individual leaves into the plastic ring, positioning a leaf between each clementine.

MISTLETOE KISSING RING

Instead of just tying a bunch of mistletoe to some strategically placed light fitting in the hall, be creative and make a traditional kissing ring. This can be hung up as a Christmas decoration and still serve as a focal point for a seasonal kiss!

scissors
7 berries-only stems winterberry
large bunch mistletoe
twine
1 twisted wicker wreath
roll of tartan (plaid) ribbon

1 Cut the stems of the winterberry into 18cm (7in) lengths. Divide the mistletoe into 14 substantial stems and make the smaller sprigs into bunches by tying with twine. Attach a branch of winterberry on to the outside of the wreath with the twine. Add a stem, or bunch, of mistletoe so that it overlaps about one-third of the winterberry, and bind in place. Bind on another stem of winterberry, overlapping the mistletoe.

2 Repeat the sequence until the outside of the cane ring is covered in a herringbone pattern of materials. Cut four lengths of ribbon of approximately 60cm (24in) each. Tie one end of each of the pieces of ribbon to the decorated ring at four equidistant points. Bring the four ends of the ribbon up above the ring and tie into a bow; this will enable you to suspend the finished kissing ring in position.

TIP
Very simple in its construction, this design does require a reasonable quantity of good quality, fresh mistletoe for it to survive the full festive season.

NUT AND CONE GARLAND

This wintry garland is very simple and quick to make.

MATERIALS

glue gun
ready-made vine garland
fir cones
brazil nuts
walnuts
hazelnuts (filberts)
red paper ribbon
stub (floral) wire

1 Using a glue gun, simply stick the various ingredients to the vine garland, beginning with the fir cones. Glue them to the ring in groups of 4–5, leaving a good space between each group. Stick larger cones to the bottom of the garland and use any smaller ones on the sides and the top.

2 Add the nuts either in groups of one variety only or mixed together. In either case, make sure that you fill the spaces between the cones to hide as much of the ring as possible. Arrange the ingredients so that they graduate from a thin layer at the top of the ring to a thicker one at the bottom.

TIP
When the garland of nuts and cones is beginning to look a little tired, you can freshen it up with a coat of spray paint. Silver, gold and white provide the most successful frosting effect because some of the natural colour of the materials in the garland will show through from underneath the paint.

3 Once all the ingredients have been added to the garland, add the finishing touches. To secure the paper ribbon in place, either pass a stub (floral) wire through the back of the knot and thread the wire through the ring, or simply glue the bow in place. For a smarter effect, you can spray the bow lightly with gold paint.

INDEX